KURTAL
Explores Australian Aboriginal Art

Research, Illustrations, and Writing by Tony Haruch

CrystalProductions
Glenview, Illinois

Library of Congress Cataloging-in-Publication Data

Haruch, Tony.
 Kurtal explores Aboriginal art / research, illustrations, and writing
Tony Haruch.
    p. cm.
 ISBN 978-1-56290-533-0
 1. Art, Aboriginal Australian—Juvenile literature. I. Title.

 N7401.H37 2007
 704.03'9915—dc22

                          2007000904

ISBN 978-1-56290-533-0
Printed in Hong Kong

HELLO!

My name is Kurtal. I'm an Australian Aborigine boy also known as the "Rainmaker Boy" because I spend a few months of every year creating a huge rainstorm we call a monsoon. I live in the town of Broome in Western Australia on the Indian Ocean, and before you follow me on my travels to show you the Aboriginal art my people create, I must fill the ponds we call "billabongs" so that all the plants and animals can come out of the ground to make our journey more pleasant.

Here, I am holding my "monsoon basket." To make it, I weave a very large basket and the little baby clouds come down to help me put it together and place it over my shoulders. Then, the big clouds pull me high up in the sky before I drop down to the ocean where I mix baskets of water and sand and cast them in the path of strong winds. I do this over and over every day for several months until the heavy rains begin. Finally, the plants and animals will be happy.

Here you can see the monsoon in action with the winds and the sand swirling every which way and you can barely see the sky for days on end. I twirl and twist my monsoon hat so that much rain falls on the dry land and keeps the Indian Ocean full of water.

The little mouthless, ghost-like heads you see twirling around are "Wandjinas." There is an ancient story that the Aborigine people tell about these people coming down from the sky during a monsoon and when it was over, they settled in a place near the ocean called the Kimberley area until they were ready to go back to the ocean and the sky. I will tell you more of their story further on in this book.

The monsoon brings great joy because on the last day of the monsoon, the plants, frogs, fish, crocodiles, and birds come out to celebrate a beautiful SUNNY day. You can see them all on the next page.

"Krock" is my favorite crocodile, and he is so happy that the monsoon is over, he went to the tanning salon to have his skin made yellow. Then, he went to the tattoo parlor and had designs made on his skin. Finally, he had extra large glasses made so he could see better when he did his dance of great joy on his favorite billabong.

The birds come out to see Krock dance, and the sleeping water lilies begin to bloom

Remember when I told you about the Wandjinas who are the mouthless ghostlike creatures who swirl around in the monsoon?

Well, they have a leader and his name is Namar. He's also a Wandjina, and he's called the big boss in the sky because he gave the Wandjina their language, culture, and law.

On the picture on the next page, Namar is represented with antenna-like shapes extending from his head. The little white circles are baby clouds to help hold him on his planet. The little black dots are magnets to keep the clouds from falling off.

And the red and white scarf around his head keeps him warm. The collage was made by an unknown Aborigine artist.

I like the smiley faces on the antennas, don't you?

Namar has his own planet and never comes down to earth. He sends messages to the ancient Wandjinas wherever they live. Do you see the little lizard on the very large rock looking up at the sky? He is very surprised to see Namar in his planet.

YOU can make a collage. All you need are colored paper scraps, some cut shapes from magazines, some colored dots, and tissue paper! And don't forget the glue! Arrange all the different pieces on a 9 x 12-inch piece of heavy paper until you like your composition, then glue each piece down carefully.

On the next page, you can see I have traveled to a cave near my home in Broome where I can see an Aboriginal painting which was framed and put there by the artist Alison Burgu for all the people in my area to enjoy. It is called *The Wandjina and the Snakes.* The snake was considered to be the one that created the first Wandjina. The long-necked turtle is considered very important because it holds the skeleton of the Wandjina. The artist has pasted some collages of Wandjina faces on the wall of the cave, too, because she wants you to know a very good story that has been used to teach children.

It says "Do not lie, do not steal, do not say bad things about people, and do not gossip. If you do, your mouths will be sealed and disappear, just like the Wandjinas."

That is certainly a very good story and pretty scary, too. Who would want to lose their mouth?

> **YOU** can make a Wandjina family by painting the "no mouths" on white paper and then painting different colors of borders around their heads. Cut each one out and arrange them on another piece of white paper, then glue them down.
>
> You and your friends can also make masks of Wandjina faces by punching a hole on either side of a cut-out Wandjina and attaching a piece of string to each side to tie on the back of your head.

I've traveled on to the middle of a desert in the Ord River Valley where there is a small town called TURKEY CREEK.

The sign I'm holding tells you all the places in town. I think the most important place is the ART GALLERY where there are many Aboriginal artworks like the one you see on the facing page which is called *The Ord River Valley* painted by Phyllis Thomas. But first, I want to tell you a very sad story about why she made this painting.

Phyllis Thomas was born and raised in the Kimberley area of Australia. When she was very young, her father was killed while he was separating some cows from a large pack of cattle. His horse stumbled on the uneven ground and landed on top of him, unfortunately killing him instantly. This painting is a memorial to Phyllis Thomas's father.

Phyllis has painted an aerial view of the country. Look at it carefully. In the center is the Ord River with two large hills on either side. Below that is the flat country where the horse accident occurred.

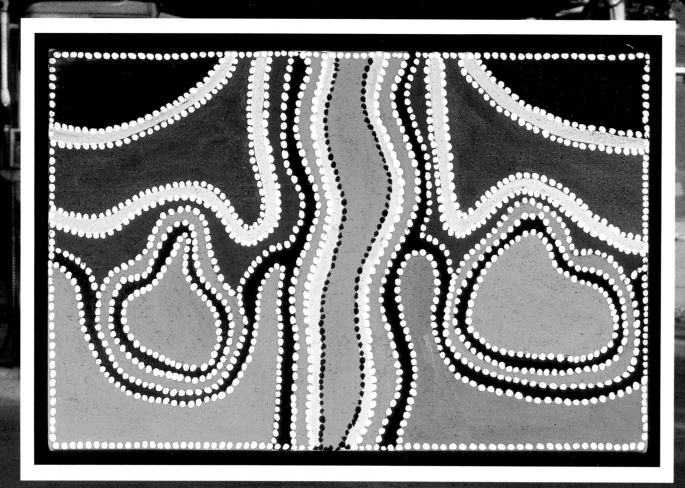

TURKEY CREEK ROADHOUSE

Food, Lodging, Gas, Store,
Post Office, Art Gallery,
Motel, Nice People

The Aboriginal painting you see on the next page is called *The Stingray* and it was painted by Dianne Tipungwuti of the Tiwi Aboriginal people. It is called an x-ray painting because the artist has painted the inside of the body of the stingray. The stingray is defined as a member of any family of large rays as having a long, whiplike tail with one or more poisonous spines that can inflict painful and sometimes deadly wounds. It is also an important food source found in the shallow waters along the Northern Territories' coastal areas in Australia.

Dianne honors the stingray by placing it as the point of interest in the painting. Her expertise in pattern-making creates an unusual composition. This shows that the Tiwi people are referred to as "pattern conscious people."

This Aboriginal painting is called *Red Fruit*. It was painted by Maryanne Tungatalum who is from the Tiwi people whose artists create paintings with beautiful designs. It is unusual to see plant forms in Tiwi art, but the red berry and fruit plants are part of the bush tucker, which means food from the wild plants. Maryanne wanted to pay respect to this red fruit that grows wild in the wooded areas. Red Bird and Blue Bird with their friend Yellow Worm are admiring the painting and also the rock patterns that Mother Nature created.

Notice the two leaves on the red fruit plant in the painting. An old Aboriginal saying about leaves says,

Leaves of one, look at some

Leaves of two, put one in your shoe

Leaves of three, leave them be (poison ivy and poison oak)

Leaves of four, hang over your door (four leaf clover)

Leaves of five, let them thrive.

YOU can create many different shaped leaves, like Mother Nature does. Draw then paint many different leaves with lines and designs on a piece of painting paper. Cut them out and you can make a round wreath or an arch for a birthday party or some other event.

I've made the journey to Kakadu Cave in Australia's Northern Territory. I've been walking in warm sun and high humidity and have worn a swimming suit so I can take a dip in the billabong right before I get to the cave. This is an interesting region of rock formations, jungles, forests, green fields, water inlets, and caves.

On the facing page, you can see two images made by ancient Aborigine artists. The one on the left is an image that has been chipped into the rock. Blue bird is telling Kurtal to watch his step. No definite meaning to this image has ever been found.

The image inside the cave is a picture of a fisherman in a boat who has been fishing for the family dinner. The bird vulture you see above him is trying to steal the fish, but the standing man is trying to keep him away.

The painting on the righthand side of the next page was made from the inside bark of a eucalyptus tree. I've shown you how the unpainted bark ready to be painted looks on the left side of the page. Preparation of the bark takes a long time and is very complicated.

Gayili Marika is the artist, and he called the painting *Story of Nandjaka*. Gayili is a painter from the Gove area of Northern Australia who enjoys using lines and shapes to symbolize the patterns of the land and the sea. The large black cone shape represents a large cloud which breaks down into small cone clouds called "Guynil." The rain from Guynil is soft and misty. It is called Nyika-Nyika and is shown as diagonal lines within the Guynil shapes. The triangular patterns represent Nandjaka, the place where the horizon meets the sea.

I decided to walk to Alice Springs to see more Aboriginal artwork, but I became so tired, I stopped to take a nap. I dreamt that I was late for my appointment, and Lemu, the emu, tells me he cannot fly but that he can run 60 miles an hour and can get me to Alice Springs in two hours. "Climb on my back and we're off!"

I asked myself, "Can he do it?" I climbed up the small ladder next to where Lemu is standing and crawled to his back and held on tightly to his feathers. "Let's go," I said.

An emu, who is a native Australian bird that cannot fly, is five feet tall and six feet long. Look how small I am standing next to him.

When Lemu and I arrived in Alice Springs, I walked to the desert region nearby where many Aborigine artists bring their artwork each weekend and sell it to art collectors and tourists who are visiting the area. The artist I especially wanted to see was Audrey Nugarri. She painted the interesting painting on the next page called *Wallaby Dreaming*. A "dreaming" is actually an Aboriginal style of painting that refers to the mythical stories and rituals passed down for generations that the artists incorporate in their paintings.

Audrey paints symbols from her culture. Look for the black digging sticks on the right and left of the center and the boomerangs or hunting sticks that appear at the top and the bottom. The circle-like shapes are campsites and watering holes connected by walkways or paths. The little figures are dancing wallabies. A real Australian wallaby is actually a small animal from the kangaroo family who only eats plants.

The old gentleman on the right is an Aborigine storyteller who helps set up the painting exhibits.

Make a picture using many different shapes and symbols. Draw shapes like boomerangs, circles, triangles, and even little figure shapes, from sheets of different colored paper. Arrange them on another sheet of paper until you have a composition you like. Then, glue them down.

I traveled next to a rock hole site near Alice Springs because I wanted to meet the Aborigine artist Bambatu Napangati who painted an artwork that represented a group of women who camped at the site to perform ceremonies before continuing their travels further east. The painting is called *Women at Rest Stop*, and you can see Red Bird, Yellow Worm, and Green Frog all looking at it.

The lines in the painting represent the sand hills surrounding the site, and the circles within circles represent water holes nearby. The women gathered large quantities of edible fruit known as pura or bush tomato from the shrubs as they passed through the area.

The carved lines you can see in the rock in the background represent trails and hunting areas.

In a rural community south of Alice Springs known as Turkey Bore, people gather at the outside studio you see on the next page to paint and chat. Most of the people are old and painting helps them forget their aches and pains. Imuna Kenta is an Aborigine artist who paints here and it is his painting called *Desert Food Menu* you see.

In the center of the painting, there is witchery grub which is found in the roots of trees and is excellent food. In each corner, Imuna painted bush plums, bush figs, and quandoms with sweet berries. On the left and right of the witchery grub is the spinifex grass that is very prickly and stinging. The people must be very careful and not brush against it.

This is the end of my journey to visit Aborigine artists and see their paintings. Someday, I'll make another monsoon and take another trip to visit more artists so I can show their artwork to you and your friends.

Friends of Kurtal say goodbye.

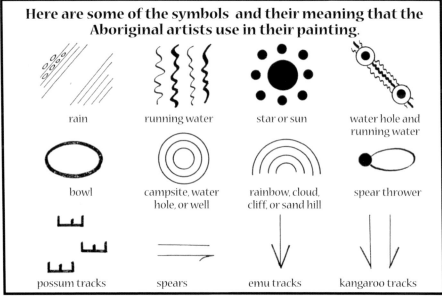

Here are some of the symbols and their meaning that the Aboriginal artists use in their painting.

rain	running water	star or sun	water hole and running water
bowl	campsite, water hole, or well	rainbow, cloud, cliff, or sand hill	spear thrower
possum tracks	spears	emu tracks	kangaroo tracks

Here are the new words Kurtal used as he told his story about his journey to find Aboriginal art:

Wandjina (wand JEE nuh) – ancient people in Derby area
billabong (BILL uh bong) – pond or low area filled with water
spinifex (SPIN ih feks) – desert grass filled with prickly thorns
bush tucker – food from wild plants
witchery grub – thick larva of certain insects found in the roots of trees that is high in protein
quandoms (qwahn dums) – wild sweet red berries
symbol (SIM bull) – a mark or drawing representing something
boomerang (BOOM e rang) – a curved flat shape thrown at an animal to stun it while hunting
wallaby – (WALL uh bee) – a small kangaroo-like animal